Best Wishes
To "all" the
Pohto's

Your neighbour
and friend

Wendy

Dec. '12

TIME TO TALK

An Interactive Experience for Adults & Children

Wendy Case

Illustrations by Iris Field

Before you get started ...some tips for comfort and conversation

Feelings are the breath and depth of life, bringing richness to the experience of living. Without feelings, we would be living in a wasteland. We can't decide to have feelings or not. But, we can certainly decide what we choose to think and feel. And, we can definitely decide how to behave based on our feelings.

Although we spend a great deal of time concerned for our children's physical, verbal, and intellectual development, often their emotional development is left to chance. In today's ever changing world, we want our children to grow up whole, strong and independent with a healthy self-esteem. To obtain this, one of the things we need to teach them is to learn to identify, trust, express and act on their feelings in a healthy way.

This book has been designed to benefit children ages 4 to 8 years old. It is meant to be used along with a most important ingredient - adult participation. It has been designed to take time to talk with the child. At the end of each story you will find questions in **red** print to ask the child in order to open conversation. The intention is to teach children about their feelings. The design of this book will allow the child to discuss their feelings with a safe and trusted adult. You!

This book is also a learning tool that can be used in everyday life with children. The underlying message that *Time to Talk* sends to children is that their feelings belong to them, their feelings are normal and can be expressed in a healthy way.

Before you introduce this book to the child, it is suggested that you put aside some time to familiarize yourself with the stories and questions in the time to talk sections. Each of the four stories represents a primary feeling (happy, angry, afraid, sad) which are the first feelings and feeling words that children learn.

At the same time, during your daily routine, try to note when your child expresses his/her feelings including the words, situations and behaviours they use. These can be areas of further conversation or reminders of 'feeling' circumstances that your child may have encountered recently. Are they only using the primary feeling words (happy, angry, afraid, sad)?

If so, try introducing the secondary feeling words to use in the appropriate situations. For example, if a child only knows the words angry or mad, what they may 'actually' be feeling is hurt, embarrassed, lonely, disappointed or jealous to name only a few. Knowing these secondary feeling words will increase their ability to understand their range of feelings.

As feelings can be such a delicate matter, it is also suggested that you read this book to a child on an individual basis. In order to show a child that you respect their feelings, ensure them privacy and confidentiality. In this way, you will learn more about their feelings. You may be surprised!

The best approach is to pick a time when you know that you will not be disturbed. Read through *Time to Talk* slowly, leaving ample opportunity to share experiences and related feelings. Inform the child that at the end of each story you will stop and talk. It is best to read one story at a time, otherwise, it may be overwhelming for the child. At first, some children may be shy but ultimately, all children want their feelings to be heard as long as they feel it is safe to do so. Listed below are some suggestions for comfortable conversations. Share your own feelings too! Build trust. Let the conversation flow by adding your own questions. At the end of the conversation, let the child know that you have enjoyed it.

Try to avoid forcing the child to talk or to share their feelings. Have a small mirror handy so that they can see their feeling faces. Let them know that all their feelings are normal and it's okay to feel that way.

★ Younger children usually don't know 'why' they are having a feeling. It is better not to ask.

★ Ridiculing or denying the child's feeling can shut them down from sharing with you. For example, "You shouldn't feel that way about grandma, she loves you. You're just tired. You don't really mean that."

★ Adult feelings are different than children's feelings which are developing and yet to be fine tuned. For example: "There's no need to be afraid of spiders, I'm not afraid."

★ Suggesting there are 'good feelings' and 'bad feelings' are limited definitions and give children a mixed message. However the behaviour used to display a feeling may be undesirable.

★ Rescuing children by trying to make their feelings 'better' for them may inhibit their emotional development. For example: "So what if your friend doesn't want to play with you, I will play with you." Again, it is normal for them to feel a range of feelings.

★ Promote using : "I feel_____ because_____and I need_____" in your family. It will diminish feuds and strengthen healthy communication if these statements are respected.

Listen: "Oh, tell me more about that feeling you are having."
Acknowledge: "I hear you are sad about _____."
Ask: "Is there something that you need right now?"

Time to Talk

This is a friendly book about a neighbourhood of children. These children are just like you except some of them may be taller or shorter, skinnier or fatter, older or younger. They may have black skin, brown skin or pink skin. They may have blue eyes, brown eyes, or green eyes.

They may even live close to your home. Maybe you know them.

This is also a book about feelings. The best part about this book is that you get to learn about your feelings and you get to talk too!

Scared   Angry   Happy   Sad

Can you name some feelings?

Feelings can be seen on faces.

Can you guess what these kids are feeling?

Feelings can also be seen on bodies.

Can you guess what this boy is feeling?

Can you buy feelings in a grocery store?

No, of course not.

Your feelings are part of who you are.

The interesting thing about your feelings is that they change all the time. One minute you can feel sad and the next minute you can feel happy. Your feelings will change and grow as you change and grow.

All feelings have names and they like to be talked about and... listened to.

YAK YAK YAK

One thing for sure is that your feelings belong to you.

**If you didn't have feelings
You wouldn't be You!**

Would you like to meet some of the kids in the neighborhood?

Hanna's house is down at the end of the block beside the playground. Her house is purple with a bright pink door with a circle on it. A scruffy dog by the name of Trouble lives at Hanna's house and guards the front door.

Can you find Hanna's house?

Arnold lives across the street from Hanna in the orange house with a sky blue door with a triangle on it. Boots, the cat, lives at Arnold's house. Boots definitely doesn't like Trouble the dog.

Can you find Arnold's house?

Sara lives in the red house with a white door with a star on it. Her yard is shaded by a giant oak tree with a tire swing hanging from it. Sara loves to play on that swing on hot summer days.

Can you find Sara's house?

Sam lives across the street from Sara in the green house with a sunny yellow door with a square on it. Sam`s mom loves to garden so his yard has flowers and vegetables of all shapes and colors.

Can you find Sam`s house?

Hanna

Hanna is a whirly-whirl kind of girl with red curly hair that stands straight up in the air. Hanna loves to dress in her party dress and pretend she is a famous dancer. Hanna is so crazy about dancing that she invents dancing shoes to match her outfits.

Sometimes she wears yogurt cups on her toes for pretend ballerina slippers. Other times, she wears blocks in her socks for pretend high heels.

Unfortunately, Hanna's shoe inventions are not very comfortable.

One day Hanna's grandmother was over for a visit and Hanna was showing off her shoe inventions.

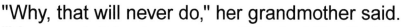

"Why, that will never do," her grandmother said. "You mustn't hurt your poor little feet like that."

The very next day, Hanna's grandmother took her shopping and bought her a brand new pair of shinny red shoes. They fit just right and were so bright they twinkled when Hanna walked.

As Hanna was sitting in the car on the way home from the store, she could feel her toes start to wiggle, her ankles start to giggle and, even her knees start to riggle. Hanna wasn't doing this on purpose, it had something to do with her new shoes. They felt like they wanted to...DANCE.

When they finally arrived home, Hanna's shoes seemed to dance out of the car all on their own. They danced up the sidewalk and into the kitchen where her mother was making lunch.

"Mom. Look at my shiny new shoes!" Hanna exclaimed.
"My toes twinkle and I cannot stop my shoes from dancing. I feel so happy."

Hanna's mom called her 'twinkle toes' all day which made Hanna grin from ear to ear.

When Hanna's dad got home from work that night, she was excited to show him how she could twirl and whirl, swing and swish, slide and glide. Oh my goodness, even bounce and flounce!

It was so easy for Hanna because her shoes did all the dancing.

Trouble barked and joined in the dance.

When Hanna put her pyjamas on that night, she begged her mom to let her wear her new shoes to bed but her mom said it wasn't a good idea. So, Hanna carefully placed her shoes under the bed so she could jump into them in the morning.

When she woke up in the morning, she swung her feet over the side of the bed to slip them on but ...

"Oh No!," her shoes were gone.

At first, Hanna tried hard not to cry but the tears came out all on there own. It was not easy to tell her mother how she was feeling... but she did.

"Oh mommy, I feel so sad," Sara sobbed. "My shoes have disappeared."
"What do you need right now Hanna?" said her mom in a soft mommy like voice.
"I need a cuddle. And, I need you to help me find my twinkle toes," Hanna said as she fell into her mother's big, soft arms.

After a long cuddle with her mom, Hanna felt better. She was glad that she told her mom how she was feeling. Later that day, after looking high and low, Hanna discovered who had taken her shoes.

Can you guess who?

Hanna was happy again because she had her twinkle toes back.
She never left them under the bed again.

Time to Talk about Happy Feelings

You probably know what it is like to feel happy. There are so many things that you can be happy about. A walk in the woods, a bowl of cherries, a cozy bed.

Can you make a happy face? (Show them your happy face)
Where does happy live in your body?
Tummy? Head? Toes? Heart?
Can you name 10 things that make you happy?
Count them on your fingers.

Another word for happy is excited.

What makes you feel excited?
Does your tummy have butterflies in it when you are excited?

Sometimes people make funny sounds when they are happy.

Do you know what these funny sounds are called?

If someone tickled your feet right now, would you make those sounds?
(Tickle, tickle)

Sometimes when we are happy we feel like being silly.

Have you ever felt like being silly?
Did you laugh and laugh?

Maybe you would like to be happy all the time but if you were happy all the time, all the other feelings inside you wouldn't have a chance to come out.

Remember, you have many other feelings too.

**If you didn't have feelings,
You wouldn't be You!**

Arnold

Even on sunny days, there was a thunderstorm hanging over Arnold's head because he was always angry. Since he was so angry, none of the kids in the neighbourhood wanted to play with him. Boots the cat didn't want to play with him either because Arnold teased and taunted her.

Boots was afraid of Arnold's new trick of trying to catch her by the tail. It hurt Boots when Arnold did this because her tail was so sensitive. Boots, of course, tried to tell Arnold how she felt about this. HISS-HISS-SWAT-SWAT but Arnold didn't seem to care.

The other kids in the neighborhood scattered when Arnold came out to play.

"Look out," they would warn each other.

"Here comes Arnold."

At first, Arnold would pretend that he was going to play nicely but then he would do things that hurt the other kids.

Like the time when he and Sara were on the teeter totter. Sara was high up in the air and Arnold pretended that he fell off.

Sara came down with a WHAM!

She not only bruised her bottom but her feelings were also hurt because she was so embarrassed.

There was no doubt. All the kids in the neighbourhood knew it. Arnold was a meany and a bully. He was nasty and always seemed to be hurting others.

What the kids didn't know was that Arnold 'couldn't ' play some of the games they played because it was difficult for him to do things that seemed easy for other kids to do. Hard things like playing trucks in the sand box.

This was why Arnold got so frustrated. Unfortunately, it always seemed to come out of him as anger.

Arnold didn't like being angry all the time but he felt jealous that the other kids could do things that he couldn't. He felt hurt inside when the kids in the playground ran away from him or pretended he was invisible. Arnold was embarrassed because he couldn't do small things with his hands. Like hanging onto the teeter totter handles. He didn't want the other kids to know that he couldn't do these things so he was mean instead.

Soon, Arnold's mother started taking him to a special place in town where a nice lady taught him how to do small things with his hands. Arnold practiced and practiced.

Soon he could grab onto his toothbrush, his dad's tennis balls, his sister's ponytail, the remote on the TV, bathtub knobs and even Boots. Boy, that was great.

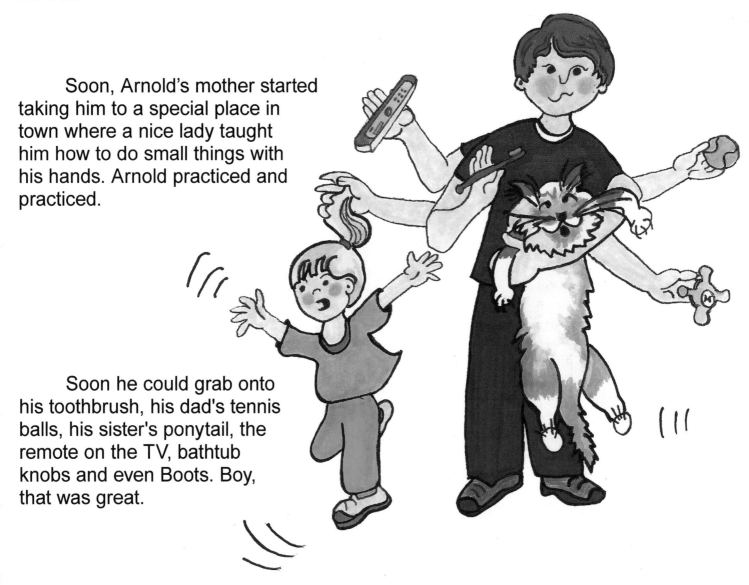

After practicing really, really hard, Arnold decided to show the kids he could now play trucks in the sand pile.

But when he tried to play, the kids were so scared of him that they ran away. Arnold felt very disappointed as he wanted so much to show them he could play nicely now.

That night, Arnold talked to his dad about his feelings. After talking, Arnold decided that maybe he could try telling the kids he was sorry for being so mean. Maybe he could promise them he would play nicely now.

Arnold practiced with Boots first.

"I am sorry for trying to pull your tail," he said, feeling rather ashamed of how he had treated Boots.

But, Boots wasn't too sure whether he could trust Arnold's new niceness.

Soon, you will find out how the kids in the neighborhood learned to trust Arnold.

Time to Talk about Angry Feelings

You probably know what it is like to feel angry. Sometimes, if someone takes your favourite toy away or bothers you when you are reading a book, you might feel angry. Another word for angry is mad.

> Can you show me your angry face?
> (Show them your angry face)
> Where do you feel anger in your body?
> Can you tell me 5 things that make you angry?

Did you know that it's okay to be angry at someone you love? It doesn't mean that you don't love them anymore, it just means that you are mad at them.

> Have you ever been angry at someone you love? Who was it?
> Do you know 'why' you were angry at them?
> What did you decide to do?

Sometimes when you are angry, you may feel like saying mean things to the person you are angry with. You might get soooooooooo angry that you want to yell or even hit them.

> Have you ever said mean things or hit someone because you were angry?
> Did this make your anger go away?
> Has anyone ever hit you because they were mad?
> How did it feel when you were hit ?

The best thing for you to do when you are angry is to take 5 long, deep breaths way down in your tummy, hold the air in and count to 5. Then, let the air out slowly like a balloon.

Let's try now! (Breathe In...count to 5...Breathe Out)

Sometimes when you are so angry and you feel like you want to explode, you can:

★ Say to the person: "I feel (tell them how you feel because (tell them why) and I need (tell them what you need)."

★ Walk away from the person and find a quiet place to be by yourself.

★ Draw a picture about how angry you are.

★ Dance how angry you feel.

★ Stomp your feet really hard.

★ Or ....maybe even run around the house a kazillion times!

Now when you are angry, you can decide what to do

**If you didn't have feelings
You wouldn't be You!**

Sara

Sara didn't like going outside to play in the summertime because she was afraid of things that started with the letter 'B.'

Bees that buzzed around and bit her.
Beetles that bashed into her bare feet.
Butterflies that breezed around her body.
Birds that tried to balance on her head.

AND.... a Big Boy with bad manners!

Arnold, who as you remember, bruised her bottom and her feelings.

As summer was nearing, Sara was worried about all the things she was scared of but knew she had to be brave. Sara thought and thought about how to solve her problem. She also asked her mom and dad for their ideas.

They suggested that she get some books from the library and learn about all the summertime B's so she could get to know them.

Finally, Sara decided to:

* ⭐ Wear dark clothes so the bees wouldn't think she was a flower.

* ⭐ Borrow her dad's big orange boots so the beetles wouldn't bash into her toes.

* ⭐ Wear her mom's big beautiful hat so the birds and butterflies wouldn't balance on her head.

This is what she looked like when she went outside.

Sara was delighted that she had found some answers to her summertime problem.

The very next day, when she looked out the window, it was sunny and warm. She saw the kids at the playground waiting for her to come out to play. Sara knew she had to be brave.

After she had been playing for awhile, she realized that she didn't feel scared anymore. Everything was working perfectly.

No bees - No beetles - No butterflies
Not even the birds bothered her.

Sara felt so proud of herself for facing her fears that she forgot that she was afraid. In fact, she felt perfectly happy building a town in the sand pile with Hanna and Sam.

Then, all of a sudden, there was a dark shadow covering the sand pile where they were playing.

Sara felt her heart start to beat fast.

Thump.Thump.Thump...

Sara felt a big knot in her tummy. She knew instantly what it was.

Sara had forgotten. She had been so concerned with the bees, butterflies, birds, boots, and beautiful hats, that she had forgotten that she was also afraid of a...

Big Bad Mannered Boy. Arnold!

"Think Sara, think," her brain told her.
"What should you do?"

Sara was frozen stiff with FEAR.

Should she:

Just start crying?
(which she felt like doing)

Should she:

Throw sand in his face?

Should she:

Run home where she felt safe?

Sara's brain reminded her that she could be courageous. She jumped up, put her hands on her hips, puffed herself up with air and pushed her shoulders back.

Then, she looked Arnold square in the eye and said,

"I'm not afraid of you anymore Arnold! No one here wants to play with you when you are mean. You can come and play nicely with us or, you can go away and play by yourself! "

"So there!"

Arnold started to get angry like he used to. Then, he remembered what he and his dad had talked about.

Arnold glanced at all the things in the sand pile to play with: cars, trucks, and roads. There was even a digger with a handle to turn. He knew he could turn that handle now.

"I'm sorry Sara. I know how to play nicely now," he said sheepishly. "I'm not mad anymore."

All the kids forgave Arnold and decided to share the sand pile and trucks with him.

Together they built an amazing town.

Time to Talk about being Afraid

You probably know what it feels like to be scared or afraid. There are many things that can make you afraid or scared: monsters under your bed, spiders in the garden, or loud thunder storms. Sometimes you can even be afraid of other people, like Arnold.
      Can you make your scared face?

Close your eyes for a minute and think about what makes you scared?
      Do you know why you were afraid?
      Was it something 'real' or 'make believe' like in a video?
      What did your brain decide to do?

Sometimes when you are afraid, you might be worried that something bad will happen.
      Have you ever felt worried?
      Can you show me your worried face?
      (show them your worried face)
      What did you decide to do when you were worried?

Sometimes when you are scared or worried, if the feeling is BIG, you need to go and talk to a special person that you trust. But, sometimes, if it is a little worry, you could decide to be brave - like Sara.
      Have you ever had to be brave?
      Was it hard to be brave?
      Then what happened?
      Did you feel proud of yourself?

      Now when you are scared you can decide what to do.

**If you didn't have feelings...
You wouldn't be You!**

Sam

Remember Sam. He spent a great deal of time feeling sad. In fact, the only time that he felt happy was when he was eating chocolate ice cream. Sam had eaten so much chocolate ice cream that his body had blown up like a balloon.

Sam was always sad because more than anything, he wanted to run and jump like the other kids in the neighbourhood but his feet felt like they were made of stone.

He wanted to ride a bike like the other kids but he kept falling off.

He also wanted to slide down the slide but he kept getting stuck at the top.

Because he couldn't do any of these things, the other kids didn't think he was much fun to play with. They called him Fatty No Fun. This hurt Sam's feelings A LOT!

Sam spent most of his time feeling lonely because the kids never wanted to play with him. So, he would spend his play time over at the nature park close to his house. He liked to kick pine cones around and talk to the squirrels who chattered back to him.

One day on the forest trail, Sam met Mrs. McGillicutty, a friend of his Mom's from the neighbourhood. She liked to run on the soft, forest trails.

"Would you like to run with me?" she asked Sam.

"I would Mrs. McGillicutty but I can't." Sam replied. "My feet are too heavy. They feel they are made of stone," he was embarrassed to tell her.

"Then, why don't we just walk together?" Mrs. McGillicutty asked.
"Sure," said Sam. "I can do that. I walk here all the time. The forest is my friend."

Sam and Mrs. McGillicutty talked about many things along the way. She knew all the names of the birds, trees and flowers along the path. They also talked about chocolate ice cream.

Mrs. McGillicutty asked him if he wanted to join her tomorrow as long as they went together to ask his Mom and Dad if it was okay. Sam knew they would think it was a good idea.

The next day came and they walked. Then, the next day came and they walked again... and again. Sam was excited that he had someone to walk with and talk to.

After many days of walking, Mrs. McGillicutty asked him if they could 'please' walk a little faster.

Sam looked over his shoulder to her and said, "I'll try but I'm not sure I can."

Sam was surprised how easy it was to walk faster. His feet didn't feel like stone anymore so he began to walk even faster and faster.

After a few days, Sam suggested to Mrs. McGillicutty that they try running for a few minutes.

Sam tried his best to run. To his surprise, running a short way was easy. After a few days, Sam ran and ran and ran.

One day Sam came running out of the forest and over to the playground beside Hanna's house. He climbed up the stairs of the slide and then came down with a SWOOSH! He jumped into the air, did a flip, landed on his feet and then, he even did a somersault.

At that very moment, Sam knew he didn't need to be embarrassed anymore.

When Sam slowed down, he noticed that Hanna, Arnold and Sara had been watching him. They were cheering at him for the splendid flip in the air. Sam beamed because he felt so proud of himself.

It seemed that all the kids wanted to play with Sam now because he was so much fun to be with. He could run, jump and even ride his bike without falling off. Sam wasn't sad anymore.

The chocolate ice cream?

Well, he decided that he only liked eating it on Saturdays.

Time to Talk about Sad Feelings

You probably know what it feels like to be sad.

Can you make a sad face? (show them your sad face)

Feeling sad can be a heavy feeling. Sometimes, it makes your body feel tired and saggy.

Sometimes you might feel sad and lonely when someone you care about has gone away and you miss them.

Can you remember a time when someone went away and you felt lonely?
What did you decide to do?

Sometimes you might feel sad and disappointed when you have no one to play with.

Have you ever felt disappointed?

Feeling sad can sometimes make you cry. Crying is good for you because it lets the sadness out.

Can you remember a time when you felt sad?
Do you know why you felt sad?
What did you decide to do?
Who could you talk to when you feel sad?

You and Sam aren't the only ones to feel sad. Everyone feels sad sometimes. Even dogs like Trouble, the shoe stealer.

It's s okay to be sad. When you are sad, you can:

★ Draw a picture of your sadness.

★ Have a good cry. ....whaaaaaaaaaaa.

★ Talk to someone you feel safe with.

★ You can say, "I feel sad because (tell the person why you feel sad) and I need (ask the person for what you need)."

Can you think of other things to decide to do when you feel sad?

When you are sad or lonely, you can decide what to do.

**If you didn't have feelings
You wouldn't be You!**

About the Creators

Wendy Case is passionate about kids! As a single parent, Wendy found herself hovering over her four year old son with a cooking spoon in her hand and her Mother's words coming out of her mouth. She decided to take the first parenting course she could find and taught parenting for many years.

Wendy completed a Degree where she focussed on child development. She worked as a social worker and taught Early Childhood development at the college level.

Iris Field is an artist and a retired educator who began her career teaching Senior Secondary Art and finished her career as an Elementary Classroom teacher.

Children of all ages have always brought great joy and wonder to her life.

Iris lives, works and has created a home with her artistic family, daughter Kaitlyn and husband Robert, in a cabin on a meadow beside the ocean.